ANNA AKHMATOVA

Requiem

and

Poem without a Hero

ANNA AKHMATOVA

Requiem

and

Poem without a Hero

translated by
D. M. THOMAS

SWALLOW PRESS ATHENS OHIO

Swallow Press
An imprint of Ohio University Press, Athens, Ohio 45701
www.ohioswallow.com
All rights reserved

Swallow Press/Ohio University Press books are printed on
acid-free paper ♾ ™

Requiem and Poem without a Hero first published in England
1976 by Elek Books Limited, London

ISBN 978-0-8040-1195-2 pbk

Library of Congress Catalog Number LC-76-7252

Contents

Acknowledgments

All translators of Akhmatova are indebted to G. P. Struve and B. A. Fillipov, editors of the only full and scholarly edition of her works: the two-volume *Akhmatova:Sochineniya* (Inter-Language Literary Associates, second edition, revised and enlarged, 1967–68). My introduction and notes to *Poem without a Hero* draw heavily on their scholarship, and also on Max Hayward's excellent introduction and notes in *Poems of Akhmatova*, selected and translated by Stanley Kunitz with Max Hayward (Collins-Harvill, 1974).

The translation of *Requiem* was first published in the *Guardian* (London), 19 April 1965. It has been revised for this book; and the author's *Dedication*, omitted from the newspaper publication, is now included.

The translation of *Evening* first appeared in *Ambit* magazine, and the two following lyrics in *The Meanjin Quarterly* (Melbourne). The Russian text of these poems can be found in the *Penguin Book of Russian Verse* (edited by D. Obolensky).

Finally I wish to thank Michael Glenny, of the Centre for Russian and East European Studies at the University of Birmingham, and Mrs Vera Dixon, for their help and advice in the preparation of *Poem without a Hero*.

D.M.T.

Poem in a Strange Language

Starlings, the burnable stages of stars,
Fall back to earth, lightly. And stars,
Propulsars of angels, die in a swift burn.
And half the angels have fallen below the horizon.

And, falling like alpha particles,
Re-charge the drowned woman
Floating in the bitter lake,
Her hair gold as their blood, her face amazed.

She is Lot's wife, her naked body
Sustained by the salt she has loosened from,
And as her eyes open, grain
Turns green-golden on the black earth of Sodom.

I enter your poem, Mandelstam, yours, Anna
Akhmatova, as I enter my love—
Without understanding anything
Except its beauty and law.

And the way its cloud of small
Movements lifts lightly the fruit
Of a painful harvest and moves
With singing vowels away from death.

D. M. Thomas

Introduction

I

Akhmatova hated the word poetess. If we call her by that
name, it is in no condescending sense but from a conviction
shared by many critics and readers that her womanliness is
an essential element of her poetic genius, a something added,
not taken away. Gilbert Frank has pointed to her unusual
blending of classical severity and concreteness with lyrical
saturation; Andrei Sinyavsky, to the range of her voice
'from the barest whisper to fiery eloquence, from downcast
eyes to lightning and thunderbolts'. No insult is intended,
therefore, in saying that Akhmatova is probably the greatest
poetess in the history of Western culture.

She was born in 1889, in Odessa on the Black Sea coast,
but her parents soon moved to Petersburg. All her early life
was spent at Tsarskoye Selo, the imperial summer residence;
her poetry is steeped in its memories, and in Pushkin, who
attended school there. In 1910 she married the poet Nikolai
Gumilev, and her own first collection, *Evening*, appeared in
1912. She and her husband became a part of that rich
flowering of creative talent—the names Blok, Stravinsky,
Diaghilev, Mendelstam Prokofiev, Meyerhold merely begin
the list—which made it the Silver Age: though it might
better be described as the second Golden Age. Akhmatova,
Mandelstam and Gumilev became the leaders of 'Acmeism',
a poetic movement which preferred the virtues of classicism,
firmness, structure, to the apocalyptic haze and ideological
preoccupations of Blok and the other Symbolists.

Gumilev was shot by the Bolsheviks in 1921 as an alleged
counter-revolutionary. Despite the fact that Akhmatova and

he had been divorced for three years, the taint of having been associated with him never left her. To borrow Pasternak's metaphor (from *Doctor Zhivago*), she had reached the corner of Silver Street and Silent Street: practically none of her poetry was published between 1923 and 1940. At the beginning of the Stalinist Terror, her son, Lev Gumilev, was arrested—released—rearrested, and sent to the labour camps. Nikolai Punin, an art critic and historian, with whom she had been living for ten years, was also arrested, though he was released a year or two later: the first lyric of *Requiem* is said to refer to his arrest. Her son was released early in the war to fight on the front-line; but he was again arrested and transported to Siberia in 1949. He was finally freed only in 1956, after Stalin's death and partial denunciation.

For Akhmatova herself, life was relatively happier during the war, when the enemy was known and could be fought. Such 'happiness', as she said, was a comment on the times! She endured the first terrible months of the Leningrad siege, and was then evacuated, with other artists, to Tashkent. Some of her poems were published, and in 1945 a collected works was said to be forthcoming. It never appeared. In the renewed repression a violent campaign of abuse was directed at her. She was too personal, too mystical. Zhdanov, Stalin's cultural hack, described her as a nun and a whore. This would appear to be a marvellous mixture of archetypes for a poet, but of course his remarks were neither meant, nor taken, in that way. She was expelled from the Writers' Union—tantamount to her abolition—and was henceforth followed everywhere by two secret police agents.

The 'thaw' following Stalin's death led to a cautious rehabilitation. Some of Akhmatova's poetry was published again, though (and this is still the case) never *Requiem*, except in isolated fragments. *Poem without a Hero*, also, has never been published complete in the Soviet Union. Granted permission to visit the West, she received the honorary degree of D.Litt. at Oxford in 1965, and revisited old friends in London and Paris. What was much more important to her than official tolerance, she had become deeply loved and revered by her countrymen. To them, she was the conscience of Russia; she had not fled to safety as others had done after the Revolution; she had chosen to stay and endure, and to 'bear witness'. She died in 1966. Five thousand people, mostly the young, crowded to her requiem mass in a Leningrad church.

The present volume is devoted to her two greatest achievements, *Requiem* and *Poem without a Hero*. Competent translations of many of her shorter poems exist, in the Kunitz-Hayward *Poems of Akhmatova*. I have however included, as an appendix, three lyrics, as examples of her poetry during the period of her life which *Poem without a Hero* recalls.

Requiem needs little introduction; it speaks for itself. It belongs to a select number of sacred texts which, like American Indian dream-poems but for more sinister reasons, were considered too momentous, too truthful, to write down. From 1935-40, the period of its composition, to 1957, it is said to have survived only in the memories of the poet and a few of her most trusted friends. It was first published in 1963, 'without the author's knowledge or consent', by the Society of Russian Emigré Writers, from a copy which had found its way to the West.

Faced with the events of the Stalinist Terror—the most monstrous epoch in human history, as Joseph Brodsky has called it—only the bravest and most complete artists can respond with anything but silence. For those few who can speak about such things, only two ways of dealing with the horror seem possible: through a relentless piling-on of detail, as Solzhenitsyn has done in *Gulag Archipelago*; or through the intensity of understatement. The latter is *Requiem*'s way. In telling us about one woman, standing in the endless queue outside a Leningrad prison, month after month, hoping to hand in a parcel or hear some news of her son, Akhmatova speaks for all Russia. She achieves universality, through an exquisiteness of style that is at the same time anonymous and transparent—the voice of 'the orphans, the widows', in Chukovsky's prophetic phrase of 1921. *Requiem* honours poetry, as well as the dead.

Though it was slowly distilled, it comes to us as a single heart-rending cry. *Poem without a Hero*, in contrast, is sustained, polyphonic, symphonic. It is a fairly long poem; nevertheless Akhmatora's preoccupation with it over so many years—from 1940 virtually until her death—is astonishing. A poem which describes possession, it possessed her. She writes: 'For fifteen years, again and again, this poem would suddenly come over me, like bouts of an incurable illness (it happened everywhere: listening to music at a concert, in the street, even in my sleep), and I could not tear myself away from it, forever making amendments or additions to a thing that was supposedly finished.' Akhmatova regarded it as her crowning achievement, the poem in which—in the words of Yeats, whom she resembles in some ways—she had 'hammered her thoughts into unity'.

The theme of the poem first came to her, she tells us, on the night of 27 December 1940, in the form of a ghostly masquerade: her friends from the Petersburg of 1913. The whole poem is a superimposition of joyous, talented, light-hearted Petersburg upon tormented Leningrad—or vice versa, since time becomes illusory, and 'mirror of mirror dreams'; a palimpsest of city upon city, the Tsarist capital erased and the Soviet city becoming so, under the German onslaught. One thing is very clear: whatever else the poem is, it is Akhmatova's love poem to her city.

That love is a positive and enriching enchantment. But the poem also relates a negative enchantment or obsession: certain personal events of 1913 which Akhmatova faces anew and, by facing them, expiates. These events are related obliquely ('Don't expect my midnight Tale of /Hoffmann to be laid bare . . .').

One of the cultural centres of pre-Revolutionary Petersburg was the Stray Dog, a basement cabaret decorated by a leading set designer, Sergei Sudeikin. It provided a stage for a constellation of poets—Blok, Bely, Kuzmin, Bryusov, Khlebnikov, Mayakovsky, Gumilev, Akhmatova, Yesenin, all read there to large audiences. There were also intimate theatrical performances. The 'events' which make up the narrative framework of Part One of *Poem without a Hero* concern three members of the Stray Dog coterie. One of them is the great Symbolist poet Alexander Blok. Akhmatova, while revering Blok as a poet, not only disliked the whole Symbolist cult but also—as becomes clear in the poem—sensed a demonism in Blok's nature.

The two other main protagonists are less celebrated. Sudeikin's wife, Olga Glebova-Sudeikina, was one of the great beauties of a city which cultivated feminine beauty. She acted and danced at the Stray Dog productions, and was a great friend of Akhmatova; they lived together in the same house for several years after the Revolution until Sudeikina emigrated to Paris in 1923. She died there shortly after the Second World War. One of her admirers in Petersburg was Vsevolod Knyazev, a young officer in the dragoons who also wrote poetry. On New Year's Eve, 1912, Knyazev discovered that Blok was his rival for Sudeikina's love, and shot himself on the stairway of her house. His pathetic and senseless death is the obsession that the poem brings into the light and 'weeps out'.

Two other characters enter the poem: Mikhail Kuzmin, described as the Aubrey Beardsley of Russian poetry; and Akhmatova herself. Kuzmin's role is of an arch-Satan. Akhmatova's is more mysterious and important; it appears that she took some of the blame for the tragedy, was involved in the affair in a way she felt guilty about. Also, she felt so close to Sudeikina that she regarded her as a 'double'. Though she was only 'pressed against the glass—frost' on the night of Knyazev's suicide, she too is guilty. Nadezhda Mandelstam has this to say about Akhmatova's preoccupation with the double: 'It was something rooted in her psychology, a result of her attitude to people—in whom, as in mirrors, she always sought her own reflection. She looked at people as one might look into a mirror, hoping to find her own likeness and seeing her "double" in everybody. . . . Apart from the element of self-centredness, it was due as well to another quality which she displayed in high degree: a capacity to become so passionately involved in others that she had the need to tie them to herself as closely as possible, to merge herself in them.'[1]

More important than the reasons for her remorse is the

[1] *Hope Abandoned* (Collins-Harvill and Atheneum).

fact that in the poem it takes on a Russia-wide significance. The 'Petersburg event' becomes, in her eyes, 'a parable for the sins of a world on which, with the outbreak of war in 1914, a long and terrible retribution began to be enacted' (Max Hayward). We see a somewhat similar parable at work in *Doctor Zhivago*, in Lara's seduction by Komarovsky; only in Akhmatova the torment and guilt are accepted as her own.

Part One of *Poem without a Hero* is in four sections. The first narrates the appearance of the unwelcome and terrifying masquerade at her apartment in the old Sheremetyev Palace on the Fontanka canal. The second describes the heroine, Sudeikina. The third is an evocation of Petersburg, as 'not the calendar—the existing/Twentieth century drew near'. The fourth relates Knyazev's death. There is a violent change of tone and mood in Part Two, which opens with the author arguing with a modern Soviet editor, who finds the poem incomprehensible and irrelevant to modern times. The real nightmare of Leningrad's present then moves into the foreground. Part Three describes Akhmatova's evacuation from Leningrad to Tashkent. In her flight from her 'dearest, infernal, granite' city, love and guilt are again mixed.

Poem without a Hero is complex; but less so, I think, than many critics imagine. Most of the apparent difficulty lies in the obscurity and privateness of the 1913 events and in the precise details of a long-dead era. Once these are sufficiently elucidated, the poem becomes no more complex than any great poem. That is, its depths are almost limitless, if one goes on exploring them, yet its surface is clear, real, ordered and beautiful, no more and no less mysterious than the view from your window.

Or than the music of Mozart. That analogy, in fact, is a particularly apt one; the poem is musical, Mozartian. From the title-page motto, a quotation from Da Ponte's libretto to Mozart's *Don Giovanni*, the poem is full of musical references. It is composed in symphonic movements. And its metre, triptychs (normally, two rhymed lines with feminine endings followed by a masculine-ended line), gives it a triple-beat rhythm of ferocious energy, dancing lyrically, demoniacally, tragically—how well it suits the masquerade theme—in one uncurbable impulse from beginning to end.

As important as the poem's fascination with doubles (Sudeikina–Akhmatova; Petersburg–Leningrad; past–future, etc.) is its use as a leitmotif of three, the magic number. Akhmatova hinted at 'threeness' being fundamental to her poem when she described it as a 'box with a triple bottom'. Often we find a major–major–minor pattern in her groups of three: Blok–Sudeikina–Knyazev, as lovers; Blok–Kuzmin–Knyazev, as poets; Knyazev-Sudeikina–mysterious guest, her dedicatees; the three portraits of Sudeikina in theatrical roles: goatlegged nymph–the blunderer–portrait in shadows; cedar–maple–lilac; Goya–Botticelli–El Greco; Chopin–Bach–'my Seventh', which may be the Seventh Symphony of Beethoven or of Shostakovich. In each of these cases, the third element is more tragic or more mysterious, like a minor chord in music. The significance of doubles and threes is suggested even in the metre, triptychs bound into pairs by rhyme.

Our constant awareness of echoes and mirror-images is enhanced—to the Russian ear at least—by innumerable echoes of earlier poets, especially Pushkin and Blok himself. The cultural interpenetration is so dense and complete that it is almost as if the poem is being written, not by an individual, but by a line of poets, a tradition. And this, of course, is a deliberate and profound contradiction of Soviet theology, which dismisses the pre-Revolutionary past as worthless.

Images of darkness, play-acting and illusion dominate Part One—phantoms, midnight, candles, dreams, and above all, masks and mirrors. This world of 1913 is glamorous and beautiful, frivolous and touched with corruption and a death which no-one believes in. Akhmatova loves this world, and scorns it. At the poem's end, after the whole marvellously created shadow world has been exorcised, the terrible truth breaks free: flying east towards Tashkent, Akhmatova sees below her that endless road along which her son, and millions of others, have been driven to the labour

15

camps. Such a tragic moment of revelation and reality exceeds all that art can do; and through her art Akhmatova shares it all with us—agony, recognition, catharsis ... 'And that road was long—long—long, amidst the/Solemn and crystal/Stillness/Of Siberia's earth.' At this climax, the poem's predominant major–minor progression is, in the deepest sense, reversed, and we are exalted, as we are at the end of *King Lear*. We feel the unmistakable presence of moral greatness as well as great art—or rather, the moral greatness is an essential condition of the artistic greatness, of the simplicity and majesty of the style.

Nadezhda Mandelstam's recent memoir, *Hope Abandoned*, amply and movingly confirms this impression of Akhmatova. The unflinchingly honest strokes of Nadezhda's pen create a portrait of a woman who, besides her genius, had gifts of life-enriching gaiety and loyalty, and a moral strength which suffering only made stronger. Mandelstam himself foresaw this—almost incredibly—even before the Revolution, when he wrote: 'I would say that she is now no ordinary woman; of her it can truly be said that she is "dressed poorly, but of grand mien". The voice of renunciation grows stronger all the time in her verse, and at the moment her poetry bids fair to become a symbol of Russia's grandeur.' His prophecy came true, in more terrible circumstances than he imagined or *could* have imagined.

II

Translations of poetry differ only in their degree of failure. The greater the original, the greater the task which cannot, in the nature of language, be discharged. When the original language is unfamiliar to most people, as Russian is, I believe the translator has another task, onerous but in a different way: to comment on the quality, as he honestly sees it, of other translations. Justice to the poet demands this, for otherwise translations of poor quality may go on being accepted, and the original author judged by them. So wise a poet as W. H. Auden, for example, said he did not understand why Osip Mandelstam was considered a great poet. 'The translations I have seen,' he said, 'don't convince me of it.' Yet Mandelstam, by general consent among readers of Russian, is one of the greatest twentieth-century poets. His translators simply have not done him justice. I owe it to Akhmatova, therefore, to look for the mote in other translators' eyes, and someone else must look for the beam in mine.

In an important recent article, the fine émigré poet Joseph Brodsky savagely criticised English-speaking translators for not respecting the formal purity of modern Russian poetry, its immense achievement in preserving its classical forms without sacrifice of content. 'Logically,' he writes, 'a translator should begin his work with a search for at least a metrical equivalent to the original form. Some translated poems indicate that the translators are aware of this. But the tension involved is too high, it excessively shackles individuality; calls for the use of an "instrument of poetry in our own time" are too strident—and the translators rush to find substitutes. This happens primarily because these translators are themselves poets and their individuality is dearest of all to them. The concept of individuality precludes the possibility of sacrifice, which from my point of view is the primary feature of mature individuality. . . . The technique used to translate from Russian ought to differ, at least visually, from the technique used to translate from Swahili and Urdu.'[1] These are stern but fair demands. Of the four translations known to me of *Requiem*, one—Robert Lowell's—fails because it is not prepared to sacrifice; two others—Richard McKane's and Robin Kemball's—because the translators have little poetic gift of their own *to* sacrifice.

McKane's translation,[2] presumably the most widely read in Britain since it is in a cheap and popular edition, is scarcely more than a literal, line-by-line translation. It fails completely to convey anything of the quality of the original. It would be useful as a prose gloss, as in the *Penguin Book of*

[1] *Beyond Consolation* (New York Review, Feb. 7, 1974).
[2] Anna Akhmatova: *Selected Poems* (Penguin Modern European Poets, 1969).

Russian Verse. But it should not purport to be a verse translation.

Lowell's version[1] is, of course, infinitely more accomplished, but it is a Lowellian imitation rather than a translation. It is too gem-hard, masculine, muscular, clever, brilliant, to be anything but a good poem by Lowell. And quite enough too, one might say! True, in a sense, but I am troubled by the feeling that *Requiem* is a different kind of poem from most of the others that Lowell has adapted so successfully. It is the voice of one particular woman in agony and the voice of the Russian people in agony. To transplant such a poem, to alter its tone to that of febrile contemporary America, is to destroy its essence. Lowell is too good a poet to have quite done that; nevertheless, his poem is not *Requiem*.

In extreme contrast, Robin Kemball[2] has the admirable intention of being completely faithful to the poet, 'to render as closely as possible the sense, the spirit, and the music of Akhmatova's *own* message (and not the translator's!) while strictly retaining the *form* (metre, line-length, rhyme-scheme) of the Russian'. Not surprisingly, his intention is unfulfilled. It is simplistic to imagine that form can be translated from one language to another, lock, stock and barrel, as though by removal van. The 'same' metre, line-length, or rhyme-scheme, tends to emerge *not* the same: translated, in the *Midsummer Night's Dream* sense. Brodsky's phrase, 'a metrical equivalent', allows for the necessary adjustments to the nature of another language and its poetics. Kemball is too true to be good, as a better poet than he would have known to be inevitable.

Stanley Kunitz's version[3] seems to me the best of the four. It is balanced, conscientious, craftsmanlike; though perhaps less successful than his translations of Akhmatova's shorter poems in the same volume: the rhymes and half-rhymes are sometimes self-consciously sought after, and the metre too constantly iambic to reflect the subtle changes of Akhma-

---

[1] *Atlantic* (October 1964).
[2] *The Russian Review* (Stanford, July 1974).
[3] *Poems of Akhmatova* (Collins-Harvill; Atlantic Monthly Press, 1974).

tova's. It is in this vital element of sound that most English translations of Russian poetry fail, as Brodsky suggests. The polysyllabic and inflected structure of Russian allows the poets vast rhythmic resources within conservative metres which would seem restricting to us; and the same features make their ubiquitous rhyming seem strangely reticent. Vast numbers of polysyllabic Russian words can rhyme, but with delicate shades of imperfectness; by comparison, English rhymes and half-rhymes—uninflected and mainly monosyllabic—are crudely obvious.

Here, as an example of the problems which challenge the translator, are four versions of the prefatory quatrain, which Akhmatova wrote in 1961. Transliterated, it reads:

Nyét, i nyé pod chúzhdym nyébosvódom,
I nyé pod zashchítoy chúzhdykh krýl,—
Ya bylá togdá s moyím naródom,
Tám, gdye moy naród, k nyeschástyu, býl.

Richard McKane:

No, not under the vault of another sky,
not under the shelter of other wings,
I was with my people then,
there where my people were doomed to be.

Robert Lowell:

I wasn't under a new sky,
its birds were old familiar birds.
They still spoke Russian. Misery
spoke familiar Russian words.

Stanley Kunitz:

No foreign sky protected me,
no stranger's wing shielded my face.
I stand as witness to the common lot,
survivor of that time, that place.

Robin Kemball:

No, not far beneath some foreign sky then,
Not with foreign wings to shelter me,—
I was with my people then, close by them,
Where my luckless people chanced to be.

McKane's version is literal, except for the last line, where
the Russian means: 'There where my people, unhappily,
were'. Ironically, he has departed from the literal sense in
the one line where a literal translation can give a faintly
Akhmatova-like echoism (there, where, were). In the
original, the poignant and ironic alliterations of *byla/byl*
(was/were) and *narod/nyeschastyu* (people/unhappily) are
perhaps more important than the end-rhymes. None of the
versions conveys the earthy proverbial power of Akhmatova's
last line, with *byl* sternly isolated by the comma. Lowell's
'they still spoke Russian' has a wit alien to the tone of the
sequence. Somewhat ironically, Kemball's version is the
deepest betrayal. His rhyme-compelled 'close by them'
fatally weakens that identity with her people that Akhma-
tova stresses, suggesting instead that she stands a little to
one side; nor did they 'chance' to be there, as though they
just happened into Russia by accident. In my own version
of this quatrain, I am not entirely happy with 'heavenly-
cope' in the first line. Literally and metrically it is close to
the Russian, but it sounds stranger in English. The trans-
lator's key unlocks one room only by locking another.[1]

To my knowledge, there is only one complete English
version of *Poem without a Hero*: by Carl R. Proffer with
Assya Humesky.[2] It is a literal version, and the translator
modestly—and accurately—disclaims any attempt at a
poetic transformation. He employs free verse (for want of a
better phrase), as does Stanley Kunitz in his more skilful
translation of Part One, section 1. I believe there is a good
case for using free verse, as the appropriate English equiva-

[1] Since writing these comments I have come across another version of
Requiem, in *Poetry from the Russian Underground*, by Joseph Langland,
Tamas Aczel and Laszlo Tikos (Harper and Row, 1973). It is, I think,
undistinguished.
[2] Ardis, Ann Arbor, 1973.

lent, in parts of *Requiem,* and I have done so. But in *Poem without a Hero,* the triptych form is so intimately bound up with the subject-matter that it seems to me essential to attempt a version of it. Without some attempt at what Akhmatova called her 'blessedness of repetition', the poem falls to pieces. If one is going to fail, one might as well fail as elegantly as possible. I have attempted to keep to the metre, and also to the pattern of feminine and masculine endings, while using assonance as an equivalent to Russian rhyme.

The Acmeists admired Coleridge's definition of poetry as 'the right words in the right order'. A translator who lacks a fundamental respect for Akhmatova's sense, her 'right words', is doomed to fail, and deserves to. Nevertheless there are times when a literal translation would actually be unfaithful to the poem's meaning. I have tried to be as faithful as possible to the letter, but not at the expense of the deeper fidelity, to the spirit.

Sometimes the liberties I have taken are with the needs and background of the English reader in mind. For example, a literal rendering of the last two lines of *Requiem* (1) would read: 'I shall go, like the wives of the Streltsy,/To howl under the Kremlin towers'. This refers to Peter the Great's household troops, who mutinied in 1698. Two thousand of them were put to death after torture. For us, even after we have turned to the notes for information, this carries no emotional impact. It would seem preferable to use an image which, for us, is more familiar and more resonant: 'I shall go creep to our wailing wall,/Crawl to the Kremlin towers'. For similar reasons I have omitted a long prefatory prose-passage (*From a Letter to N.*) in *Poem without a Hero,* as largely irrelevant except in a Russian context, as well as some of the subtitles and literary epigraphs with which Akhmatova liberally introduces each section of her work. To purists who may argue that this is a betrayal of the text, I can only reply that I have tried always to imagine how Akhmatova might have wished her poem to be presented, in an English translation, for English-speaking readers.

D.M.T.

Requiem

No, not under a foreign heavenly-cope, and
Not canopied by foreign wings—
I was with my people in those hours,
There where, unhappily, my people were.

In the fearful years of the Yezhov terror I spent seven-
teen months in prison queues in Leningrad. One day
somebody 'identified' me. Beside me, in the queue,
there was a woman with blue lips. She had, of course,
never heard of me; but she suddenly came out of that
trance so common to us all and whispered in my ear
(everybody spoke in whispers there): 'Can you describe
this?' And I said: 'Yes, I can.' And then something
like the shadow of a smile crossed what had once been
her face.

1 April 1957, Leningrad

Dedication

The mountains bow before this anguish,
The great river does not flow.
In mortal sadness the convicts languish;
The bolts stay frozen. There's someone who
Still feels the sunset's glow,
Someone who can still distinguish
Day from night, for whom the fresh
Wind blows. But we don't know it, we're obsessive,
We only hear the tramp of boots, abrasive
Keys scraping against our flesh.
Rising as though for early mass,
Through the capital of beasts we'd thread.
Met, more breathless than the dead,
Mistier Neva, lower sun. Ahead,
Hope was still singing, endlessly evasive.
The sentence! and now at last tears flood.
She'd thought the months before were loneliness!
She's thrown down like a rock.
The heart gives up its blood.
Yet goes . . . swaying . . . she can still walk.
My friends of those two years I stood
In hell—oh all my chance friends lost
Beyond the circle of the moon, I cry
Into the blizzards of the permafrost:
Goodbye. Goodbye.

Prologue

In those years only the dead smiled,
Glad to be at rest:
And Leningrad city swayed like
A needless appendix to its prisons.
It was then that the railway-yards
Were asylums of the mad;
Short were the locomotives'
Farewell songs.
Stars of death stood
Above us, and innocent Russia
Writhed under bloodstained boots, and
Under the tyres of Black Marias.

I

They took you away at daybreak. Half wak-
ing, as though at a wake, I followed.
In the dark chamber children were crying,
In the image-case, candlelight guttered.
At your lips, the chill of an ikon,
A deathly sweat at your brow.
I shall go creep to our wailing wall,
Crawl to the Kremlin towers.

2

Gently flows the gentle Don,
Yellow moonlight leaps the sill,

Leaps the sill and stops aston-
ished as it sees the shade

Of a woman lying ill,
Of a woman stretched alone.

Son in irons and husband clay.
Pray. Pray.

3

No, it is not I, it is someone else who is suffering.
I could not have borne it. And this thing which has
    happened,
Let them cover it with black cloths,
And take away the lanterns . . .
                          Night.

4

Someone should have shown you—little jester,
Little teaser, blue-veined charm-
er, laughing-eyed, lionised, sylvan-princessly
Sinner—to what point you would come:
How, the three hundredth in a queue,
You'd stand at the prison gate
And with your hot tears
Burn through the New-Year ice.
How many lives are ending there! Yet it's
Mute, even the prison-poplar's
Tongue's in its cheek as it's swaying.

5

For seventeen months I've called you
To come home, I've pleaded
—O my son, my terror!—grovelled
At the hangman's feet.
All is confused eternally—
So much, I can't say who's
Man, who's beast any more, nor even
How long till execution.
Simply the flowers of dust,
Censers ringing, tracks from a far
Settlement to nowhere's ice.
And everywhere the glad
Eye of a huge star's
Still tightening vice.

6

Lightly the weeks are flying,
What has happened, I can't take in.
Just as, my dearest, the white
Nights first watched you in prison,
So they again gaze down
With their warm aquiline eyes and
Of your cross transcendent
And of death I hear them speak.

7

The Sentence

Then fell the word of stone on
My still existing, still heaving breast.
Never mind, I was not unprepared, and
Shall manage to adjust to it somehow.

Thank God, I've many things to do today—I
Need to kill and kill again
My memory, turn my heart to stone, as
Well as practise skills gone rusty, such

As to live, for instance . . . Then there's always
Summer, calling out my Black Sea dress!
Yes, long ago I knew this day:
This radiant day, and this empty house.

8

To Death

You will come in any case, so why not now?
Life is very hard: I'm waiting for you.
I have turned off the lights and thrown the door wide open
For you, so simple and so marvellous.
Take on any form you like.
Why not burst in like a poisoned shell,
Or steal in like a bandit with his knuckleduster,
Or like a typhus-germ?
Or like a fairy-tale of your own invention—
Stolen from you and loathsomely repeated,
Where I can see, behind you in the doorway,
The police-cap and the white-faced concierge?
I don't care how. The Yenisei is swirling,
The Pole Star glittering. And eyes
I love are closing on the final horror.

9

Already madness trails its wing
Decisively across my mind;
I drink its fiery wine and sink
Into the valley of the blind.

I yield to it the victory:
There is no time, there is no room
Except to sue for peace with my
—However strange—delirium.

I fall upon my knees, I pray
For mercy. It makes no concession.
Clearly I must take away
With me not one of my possessions—

Not the stone face, hollow blanks
Of eyes, my son's, through pain's exquisite
Chisel; not the dead's closed ranks
In the hour of prison visits;

Not the dear coolness of his hands;
Nor, dimmed in distance's elision,
Like limetrees' shady turbulence,
His parting words of consolation.

Crucifixion

'Mother, do not weep for Me,
who am in the grave.'

I

Angelic choirs the unequalled hour exalted,
And heaven disintegrated into flame.
Unto the Father: 'Why hast Thou forsaken . . .!'
But to the Mother: 'Do not weep for me . . .'

II

Magdalina beat her breast and wept, while
The loved disciple seemed hammered out of stone.
But, for the Mother, where she stood in silence,—
No one as much as dared to look that way.

Epilogue

I

There I learned how faces fall apart,
How fear looks out from under the eyelids,
How deep are the hieroglyphics
Cut by suffering on people's cheeks.
There I learned how silver can inherit
The black, the ash-blond, overnight,
The smiles that faded from the poor in spirit,
Terror's dry coughing sound.
And I pray not only for myself,
But also for all those who stood there
In bitter cold, or in the July heat,
Under that red blind prison-wall.

II

Again the hands of the clock are nearing
The unforgettable hour. I see, hear, touch

All of you: the cripple they had to support
Painfully to the end of the line; the moribund;

And the girl who would shake her beautiful head and
Say: 'I come here as if it were home.'

I should like to call you all by name,
But they have lost the lists. . . .

I have woven for them a great shroud
Out of the poor words I overheard them speak.

I remember them always and everywhere,
And if they shut my tormented mouth,

Through which a hundred million of my people cry,
Let them remember me also. . . .

And if ever in this country they should want
To build me a monument

I consent to that honour,
But only on condition that they

Erect it not on the sea-shore where I was born:
My last links there were broken long ago,

Nor by the stump in the Royal Gardens,
Where an inconsolable young shade is seeking me,

But here, where I stood for three hundred hours
And where they never, never opened the doors for me.

Lest in blessed death I should forget
The grinding scream of the Black Marias,

The hideous clanging gate, the old
Woman wailing like a wounded beast.

And may the melting snow drop like tears
From my motionless bronze eyelids,

And the prison pigeons coo above me
And the ships sail slowly down the Neva.

Poem without a Hero

a triptych

1940 – 1962

Leningrad – Tashkent – Moscow

Di rider finirai
Pria dell'aurora

Don Giovanni

Foreword

Deus conservat omnia

motto on the coat of arms of the
House on the Fontanka

Some are no more, others are distant . . .

The poem first came to me, in the House on the
Fontanka, on the night of 27 December 1940, though
I had been forewarned by a brief fragment the previous
autumn. I did not summon it, I did not even expect it,
on that cold and dark day of my last winter in Leningrad.

That night I wrote '1913' and a dedication. Early in
January I wrote, almost to my surprise, 'Obverse'; and
later, in Tashkent, 'Epilogue', which was to become
part three, together with some important additions to
the first two parts. I continued to work on the poem
after my return to Leningrad on 1 June 1944.

I frequently hear of certain absurd interpretations of
Poem without a Hero. And I have been advised to make
it clearer. This I decline to do. It contains no third,
seventh, or twenty-ninth thoughts. I shall neither
explain nor change anything. What is written is
written.

I dedicate the poem to the memory of its first audi-
ence—my friends and fellow citizens who perished in
Leningrad during the siege. Their voices I hear, and I
remember them, when I read my poem aloud, and for
me this secret chorus has become a permanent justifi-
cation of the work.

Dedicatory Poems

I

in memory of Vs.K.

. . . .
Having run out of paper,
I am writing on your rough draft.
And a word which is not mine
Occasionally shows through
Only to melt, trustingly, without reproach,
As snowflakes, once, on my hand.
And the dark eyelashes of Antinoüs
Lifted suddenly—and the green smoke
And our native breeze gently blew . . .   10
Isn't it the sea?
       No, it's only graveyard
Pine-needles, and in a boiling of foam,
Still closer, closer . . .
           Marche funèbre . . .
                   Chopin . . .

2

to O.A.G-S.

Is it you, my blundering Psyche,
Waving your black-and-white fan,
Who lean over me?
Do you wish to tell me in secret   20

You've already crossed the Lethe
And are breathing another spring?
You needn't tell me, I can hear it:
A warm downpour is pressing on the roof,
I hear whispering in the ivy.
Someone small has made up his mind to live,
Has turned green—tomorrow, fluffed up,
Will try to strut in a new cloak.
I sleep—
She alone leans over me,   30
She whom people call spring
I call loneliness.
I sleep— I dream
Of our youth.
That cup which passed him by
I'll give you, if you wish, as a keepsake:
Like a pure flame in clay,
Like a snowdrop in a grave.

3

I have frozen enough with terror,
Better summon up a Bach chaconne,   40
And behind it will come a man
Who won't become my husband, yet together
We shall deserve such things
That the twentieth century will stand agape.
He will be late, this foggy night,
Coming to drink the new year wine
In the palace on the Fontanka.
And he will remember the epiphany,
Maple at the window, wedding candles,
A poem's deathly flight . . .   50
But he will bring me, not a ring,
The first lilac nor that other sweetness, prayer—
Doom is the gift he'll bring.

RAISED HIGH, THE NINETEEN-FORTIETH YEAR
IS A TOWER. I CAN SEE ALL.
I'M SAYING GOODBYE, AS IT WERE,
TO WHAT I HAVE LONG ABANDONED;
CROSSING MYSELF, AND DESCENDING
UNDER THE DARK VAULTS OF BURIAL.

—Leningrad under siege
25 August 1941

PART ONE

The Year Nineteen Thirteen

I

New Year's Eve. The House on the Fontanka. Instead
of her expected guest, the author is visited by shadows
from the year 1913, disguised as mummers. A white
hall of mirrors. Lyrical digression: 'A visitor from the
future'. Masquerade. A poet. A ghost.

I have lit my sacred candles,   60
    One by one, and with your absent
        Companionship I hallow
            The coming forty-first year.
But . . .
        God grant us his power!
    In crystal the flame is drowning,
        'And the wine, like poison, burns.'
Malicious conversations,
    The resurrection of ravings,
        Though the hour has not yet struck . . .   70
No measure in my terror,
    I'm a shadow on the threshold
        Defending my last peace.
I listen to the insistent
    Doorbell, cold mist on
        My skin. I'm stone. Ice. Fire . . .

I half-turn, as if stricken
    By memory, as if my distant
        Voice is saying, 'You're wrong:
This isn't the Doge's Palace.   80
    It's next door.   But your masks and
        Cloaks, your sceptres and your crowns,
Leave them in the hall.   Welcome!
    Animate the New Year revel:
        It's you I celebrate.'
Here's Faust—and here's Don Juan,
    John the Baptist, Dapertutto,
        Dorian Gray; and here's the frugal
            Most northerly of the satyrs,
                Glahn. They whisper their Dianas   90
                With phrases learnt by rote.
                    Here's somebody trailing Pan—a
                    Faun with the legs of a goat.
And for them the walls have widened,
    Lights cascading, sirens whining,
        A cupola is bursting the roof.
Publish the whole scandal!
    What to me are Hamlet's garters!
        The whirlwind of Salome's dancing,
            The tread of the Iron Masker!   100
                I am more iron than they . . .
Whose turn is it now to blench with
    Fear, back away, surrender,
        Ask mercy for an ancient sin? . . .
Clearly it's
                it's me they seek—crazy!
    I've denied them, and my table
        Is set for someone else.
A tail under a dress-suit . . .
    How lame yet elegant . . .   110
                However . . .
        The Prince of Darkness: whoever
            Would dare to bring him here?
Mask, or skull, or face, his
    Expression of malice and ache I

Doubt even Goya could paint.
The suavest and the sickest,
   Compared with whom what sinner
     Is not incarnate grace?
Enough! Join in the dancing!   120
   But by what necromancy
     Am I living and they dead?
In the morning I shall waken,
   Nobody here to blame me,
     Straight into my face the
       Blue will laugh through the pane.
But now I'm frightened. I have
   Got to present myself, smile at
     Them all and fall silent,
       Hugging my lace shawl.   130
She who was I, in her black agate
   Necklace—till the valley of God's anger
     Bring us together, I'd rather
       She kept out of my way . . .
Are the last days close upon us?
   Your lessons I have forgotten,
     Sloganwriters, false prophets,
       You haven't forgotten me.
As in the past the future is maturing,
   So the past is rotting in the future—   140
     A terrible carnival of dead leaves.

A sound of steps of those not here
Over the gleaming parquet. Blue
Cigar-smoke.   All the mirrors show one who
Would not gain entry if he should appear.
No better, no worse, than others—but frigid
Lethe's not touched him, and his hand is warm.
Guest from the future, will he really come,
Taking the left turn across the bridge?

From childhood I have feared mummers.   150
   It always seemed to me that someone,
     A kind of extra shade

'Without face or name', has slipped in
  Among them . . .
           Shall we begin by
    Calling the roll on this
Triumphal New Year's Day!   But
  Don't expect my midnight Tale of
    Hoffmann to be laid bare . . .
               Wait!   You!   160
Your name's not here, I don't see it
  Among the Magi, Cagliostros, Messalinas,
    You come in the motley stripes
Of a milepost, that brilliant mask the
  Snow wears.   You . . . old as the Mamre
    Oak, interlocutor of the moon.
Your feigned groans, they cannot
  Fool us.   You write iron commandments;
    Solon, Lycurgus, Hammurabi,
      Should sit down at your feet.   170
His extraordinary nature
  Doesn't wait for gout and fame to
    Arrive in a heat and raise him
      To a pompous jubilee chair.
But over the flowering heather
  And over wildernesses
    He bears his triumph.   And
He's not even guilty of bending
  Any law . . .
           Besides, in general,   180
  Poets are blind to sin,
They must dance before the Ark of
  The Covenant, or perish! . . .
            But that's apparent
  In their verses, I'll hold my peace.
We only dream it's cock-crow.   The
  Neva is billowing with smoke.   Night
    Is fathomless.   The sabbat goes on
      And on in Petersburg . . .
In narrow windows the stars are   190
  Muffled in shrouds of disaster

But the liquid tongues of the maskers
　　Run lightly through their shames.
A shout:
　　　　　'The hero's on stage!'　Ah
　Yes, here he comes, displacing
　　The tall one without fail and
　　　Of holy vengeance he sings.
—But why have you all fled, as
　Though to a communal wedding,　　　　　　　　200
　　Leaving me in the gloom
Face to face with a frame's blackness
　Out of which stares that hour
　　Which became most bitter drama
　　　Never sufficiently wept.

It floods me not all at once
But like a musical phrase.
I hear a whisper: 'Goodbye!
I shall leave you behind,
But you will be my widow,　　　　　　　　210
You, my dove, my sun, my sister!'
On the landing, two locked shadows . . .
Then, down the broad stairs,
A scream: 'Don't do it!' Far off
A pure voice:
　　　　　'I am ready for death.'

The torches go out, the ceiling lowers. The white hall
of mirrors becomes the author's room. Words from the
darkness:

Clearly, there's no death.　Saying
　What's clear to all is banal.
　　I'd like it explained to me.
　　　　　　　　That knock!　　　　　　　　220
I thought they were all within.　Is
　This the guest from behind the mirror,
　　The shape that flitted past the pane?

Is the new moon playing a joke, or
  —Between the cupboard and the stove—is
    Somebody standing again?
Pale forehead, open lids, this
  Means that gravestones are brittle,
    That granite is softer than wax . . .
Crazy, crazy, crazy! From such crazes   230
  I shall soon be turning grey or change to
    Something else. Why
Are you beckoning me near?

          For one moment of peace here
          I would give up the grave's peace.

              Across the Landing

                (Intermezzo)

'Surely you've heard, it's all over . . .
  You're a baby, Signor Casanova . . .'
    'See you at Isaac's at six . . .'
'We'll find you somehow in the fog,
  We've promised to call at the Dog . . .'   240
    'How about you?'—
              'God knows!'
Don Quixotes, Sancho Panzas,
  Alas, Sodom's celebrants are
    Stumbling, death's wine flows.
Foam-borne Aphrodites risen,
  Helens shivering in the mirror,
    And the age of dementia moves
Nearer. From Fontanka's grotto,
  Weary of his burning-glass, love   250
    Cools and through a horn-gate passes,
      And someone ginger and shaggy
        Leads out the goat-footed nymph.

Brightest star of the scene, though
    Her mask prevents her from seeing,
        Hearing, praying, cursing, breathing,
            Is the head of Madame de Lamballe.
But you, our beauty, our joker,
    Spinning to the whim of the goatking,
        Your lisp is tender and soulful: 260
'Que me veut mon Prince Carnaval?'

Simultaneously in the depths of the hall, stage, hell—or
the summit of Goethe's Brocken—*she* appears (or
perhaps it is her shadow):

Horns in her pale curls, shoes are
    Beating a rhythm of hoofbeats,
        Drunk with the oceanic dance—
As if from a figured vase she
    Goes whirling towards the azure
        Wave, in naked elegance
And earrings ringing like sleighbells.
    And you, in helmet and greatcoat,
        Behind, who bare-faced came here,   270
            You, Ivanushka of the fable,
                What wearies you today?
So much bitterness in each word,
    Over your love so black a cloud,
        And why does that streak of blood
            Rip the petal of your cheek?

2

The heroine's bedroom. A wax candle is burning. Over
the bed are three portraits of the mistress of the house
in various roles. On the right, the goatlegged nymph;
in the centre, the blunderer; on the left a portrait in
shadows. Some might think it Columbine; others,
Donna Anna from 'The Steps of the Commendatore'.
Outside the mansard window piccaninnies are playing
snowballs. A blizzard rages. New Year's Night. The
blunderer comes alive, glides from the portrait, and
she hears a voice reading aloud:

My dove, throw wide your satin
　　Cloak!　And don't be angry
　　　That I have touched this chalice:
　　　　I condemn myself, not you.　　　　　280
It is time to settle old scores
　　—Look, in the grainy storm
　　　Meyerhold's blackamoors
　　　　Are romping about again.
And round us is Peter's creation
　　That flayed the hide of the nation
　　　(As the nation expressed it then).
In manes, harnesses, meal-carts,
　　In the variegated tea-rose,
　　　And under raven-wing clouds.　　　　290
With the image of a smile, our
　　Mariinsky prima, our dying
　　　Ineffable swan is flying,
　　　　And the late snob enters loud.
Orchestral sounds from that other
　　World, something's shadow flashed somewhere
　　　—Has the dawn already fluttered
　　　　A premonition along the rows?
And again our glory and wonder,
　　The voice like an echo of thunder,　　　300
　　　Chaliapin, throws

48

All the heart's electric,
   Riding over the land that bred him,
     All its unridable ways.
Branches in the blue-white snow . . .
   Who walks the twelve colleges' corridor now
     Will dream that he is walking through
       An echo of all that's happened, so
         Endless it is, hollow and straight.
Absurdly close, the finale: 310
   From behind screens, the mask of
     Petrushka, coachmen round fires dance, the
       Palace flies a yellow-black flag.
Everything's here that we need.   The
   Fifth and final act breathes from
     The Summer Garden . . . Tsushima's
       Hell is here.   —A drunken sailor sings.
Fly, shadows! —your sleigh-runners
   A-jingle, the she-goat's sleigh-rug a-
     Trail! —He's here alone.   320
Sharp shadow on the wall, face of
   Mephistophilis or Gabriel—
     My lady, your paladin?
Demon with the smile of Tamara,
   What are the secrets of charm in
     That terrible smoky face?
Flesh dragged towards spirit as a rock
   Quarried for the sculptor's block—
     All mystery, all outer space.
He, was it, through the packed hall,   330
   Sent you (or was it a dream?) a champagne-
     Glass containing a black rose?
With dead heart, dead expression,
   He met the commendatore, stepping
     Heavily into the cursed house.
He, was it, who first mentioned
   How you were both in a dimension
     Outside the laws of space and time—
There, in what polar crystals,
   And in what amber glister,   340

At the Lethe's—at the Neva's—mouth.
Out of the portrait you ran,
    And until the rising sun
        The frame will wait on the wall.
So dance now—dance, unescorted.
    If you crave a fatal chorus
        I consent to the role.

Scarlet spots on your cheeks;
You'd better return to the canvas.
But tonight is the kind of night   350
When accounts must be settled . . .
Yet this intoxicating drowsiness
Is harder to fight than death.

From nowhere you came to Russia,
    O my blond-haired wonder,
        Our second decade's columbine:
Why do you gaze so sharply and sadly,
    Petersburg doll and actress,
        You, my double, my twin.
Yes, write that title below your   360
    Others.   Companion of poets,
        I inherited one of your crowns.
In the divinely musical metre
    Of Leningrad's keen wind,
        In the shade of a protected cedar,
            I see a dance of courtly bones.
The wedding candles gutter,
    Veiled shoulders are kissed, a thunder
        Of church commands: 'Dove, alight!'
A meeting in a Maltese chapel,   370
    Parma violets heaped in April
        Like a curse within your heart.
Vision of the golden age, or
    A black crime in the chaos
        Of our dreadful former years?

Tell me this at least:
                              did you
        Really, at some moment, live, your
                Tiny feet gliding on air
                    While others trod the paved squares?   380
Your house like a carnival wagon,
        Peeling cupids standing
                At the alter of Venus on guard.
Your singing birds free as larks, you
        Furnished your bedroom like an arbour,
                —Who'd recognise this rustic maid?
Hidden in the walls are spiral
        Staircases; saints on the sky-blue
                Walls . . . Stolen goods . . . but all in bloom
Like the Spring of Botticelli,   390
        You received your friends in
                Bed, and your languishing dragoon
Pierrot who wore the smile of
        An evening sacrifice, that
                Most religious of your admirers—
                    You were a magnet to his steel.
He's white, the tears are flowing,
        He sees you showered with roses,
                And his rival's revered by all.
I cannot see your husband.   400
        The fortress clock has struck.   I
                Am pressed against the glass—frost.
I don't chalk crosses on houses,—
        Step bravely to this encounter—
                Long ago your horoscope was cast.

In Petersburg we'll gather again,
Around the grave where we buried the sun.

Mandelstam

Petersburg, 1913. Lyrical interlude: last recollection in
Tsarskoye Selo. A wind, reminiscent or prophetic,
mutters:

Bonfires cooked the geese of Christmas,
   Carriages toppled from bridges,
      The whole funereal city swam
On a blind assignation
   Down the Neva or against it   410
      —Only away, away from its graves.
All its arches were throbbing black molars,
   The Summer Garden's vane was crowing
      Thinly, a bright moon turned a colder
         Silver over the silver age.
Since, along all roads and
   Towards all thresholds, slowly
      A shadow advanced, the wind
Was ripping posters off the
   Walls, smoke whirled in cossack   420
      Dances on the roofs,
Lilac breathed a graveyard smell, and
   The city, demented and dostoyevsky,
      Wrapped itself in its fog.
Peter, old genius, old assassin,
   Stared again out of blankness,
      Beat an execution drum . . .
And always, something not thunder
   Under the profligate frost, a rumble
      Of war before it began.   430

But then it was heard so faintly
   It scarcely touched the ear, as flakes to
     The Neva's drifts it drowned.
As though, in night's terrible mirror
   Man, raving, denied his image
     And tried to disappear,—
While along the embankment of history,
   Not the calendar—the existing
     Twentieth century drew near.

And now to go home, swiftly,   440
Through the Cameron gallery,
To the icy mysterious park,
Where the waterfalls are silent,
Where I must make all nine glad
As once I was dear to you.
Beyond the park, beyond the island,
Can it be that our eyes won't
Meet with their clear former gaze?
Won't you really ever whisper
To me again that word which   450
         kills
           death
   And is my life's one clue?

4

The corner of Mars Field. A house built early in the
nineteenth century by the brothers Adamini. In the
bombing of 1942 it will suffer a direct hit. A bonfire
flames high. The sound of bells pealing from the Church
of the Saviour on the Blood. In the square through a
snowstorm, the apparition of a court ball. Silence itself
speaks, in the lulls between these sounds:

> Who stands stiff at the dimmed windows, on his
>   Heart that 'blonde curl',
>   Total darkness before his eyes?
> 'Help me! It's not too late! I
>   Have never seen you, night, so strange, so
>   Frosty!' The wind, deranged,
> Laden with cargoes of salt . . . It's   460
>   Not the Champs de Mars but the Baltic.
>   Invisible hooves ring . . .
> His agitation cannot be sounded
>   Whose whole life is running aground and
>   Whose only prayer's for a boundless
>   Forgetting and forgotten sleep.
> He, roaming beyond midnight under
>   Those corner windows; dully
>   A street light points at him.
> His wait is rewarded . . . An elegant masker   470
>   On the road back from Damascus
>   Is coming home . . . she's not alone.
> Someone with her without face or
>   Name . . . Unappeasable separation
>   He saw through the oblique
> Bonfire flames.   Then houses fell and
>   Produced a sobbing echo:
>   'I shall leave you behind,
> O my dove, my sun, my sister,
>   But you will be my widow,   480
>   And now . . . Goodbye. It's time.'

The landing's drugged with perfume,
　　And a cadet dragoon with verses
　　　And senseless death in his breast
Will ring, if his courage suffices,
　　That he may waste one final
　　　Moment glorifying you.
　　　　　　　　　Behold:
Not on the cursed marshes of Mazur,
　　Not on Carpathia's azure　　　　　　　　490
　　　Peaks— in your own house!
　　　Blocking the door! . . .

　　　Et te conservet Deus.

　　　　So many ways for a poet to die,
　　　　Stupid child, to choose this one,—
　　　　Couldn't endure the first hurt,
　　　　Ignorant on what threshold
　　　　He stood, the opening view
　　　　Of what road.

And it was I, your ancient　　　　　　　　　500
　　Conscience, found the burnt pages
　　　Of a story, in his home,
　　　　Placed on the edge of a sill
　　　　The dead boy's will
　　　　　And on tiptoe left the room.

ALL IS IN ORDER: THE POEM LIES
AND, AS IS NATURAL TO IT, RESTS.
BUT WHAT IF, SUDDENLY, THE THEME ESCAPES

AND HAMMERS ON THE WINDOW WITH ITS
   FISTS,—
ANSWERED BY DISTANT, DREADFUL
   SOUNDS—   510
A CLICKING IN THE THROAT, A RATTLE,
AND A VISION OF CROSSED HANDS . . .

PART TWO

Obverse

My future is in my past

I drink the water of Lethe,
My doctor won't allow me depression

Pushkin

The House on the Fontanka, 5 January 1941. Through the window the ghost of a snow-covered maple. The devilish harlequinade has just rushed by, disturbing the silence of the soundless age, and leaving behind the disorder common to all festive or funeral processions—torch-smoke, scattered flowers on the floor, holy relics forever lost . . . A wind howls in the chimney, and in this howl may be divined snatches of Requiem, deeply and cunningly hidden. Of what appears in the mirrors, it is better not to think.

I

My editor showed displeasure,
   Pleaded sickness, pleaded a deadline,
   Then, restricting his phone,
  Grumbled: 'It's got to be simpler!
   You read, and when you've finished
   You still don't know who's in love

II

With whom, who met and why, who
  Lived and who died, who's   520
    Author and who's hero.   And
Ideologically it's outmoded,
  This carrying-on about a poet
    And a swarm of ghosts.'

III

I answered: 'There were three—
  A milepost was the chief,
    Another like the devil was dressed.
Behind them their poems labour
  To help them achieve the ages.
    The third, at twenty, was dead,   530

IV

And I pity him.' And again
  Word fell out over word,
    The music box droned on.
And the clever poison flamed
  Over that bottle-hard
    Angry and corkscrew tongue.

V

I dreamt that I was held to
  Creating a libretto
    For music that flowed evermore.
And a dream—is something substantial,   540
  The Blue Bird, the soft embalmer,
    The ramparts of Elsinore.

VI

And I myself was not glad
  To receive that harlequinade,
    To hear that distant scream.

I kept hoping that like puffs of
   Smoke pine-needles would be gusted
      Past the white hall, through the gloom.

VII

With such an elegant Satan
   —So colourful—this motley ancient   550
      Cagliostro, you can't resist.
It goes against his belief
   To mourn the dead, for grief
      And conscience do not exist.

VIII

Well . . . it doesn't smell of a Roman
   Carnival.   Over the closed domes a
      Melody of cherubim
Trembles.   No-one is hammering on my
   Door, only the stillness watches
      Over stillness, mirror of mirror dreams.   560

IX

And with me is my 'Seventh',
   Mute, half-dead, a
      Puckered grimace its mouth,
That could be the mouth of a tragic
   Mask, but for the black daub,
      The stuffed-in dry earth.

X

. . . .
. . . .
. . . .

And the decades pass: tortures,   570
   Exile, executions—*you're* not
      Surprised that I can't sing.

XI

And especially when our dreams imagine
   All that must still be enacted:
      Death everywhere—our city burnt through . . .
And Tashkent in flower for a wedding . . .
   Very soon the asiatic wind will tell me
      What is eternal and true.

XII

XIII

Shall I be melted to a state hymn?
   I don't want, don't want, a diadem
      From a dead poet's brow.
The time will come for my lyre,
   But Sophocles we need, not Shakespeare.
      Fate is the night-visitor now.   590

XIV

And the theme that came
   Was a crushed chrysanthemum
      On the floor when the coffin has passed.
Between memory and call-to-mind is
   The distance of Luga's ice-fields
      From the land of the satin half-mask.

XV

The devil made me rummage . . .
   Yet how is it, I wonder,
      I am so steeped in guilt?

I of the quiet, simple manner,   600
 I the 'White Flock' and the 'Plantain' . . .
  How, my friends, excuse my fault?

XVI

If it is so confused it's
 Because I don't hide my confusion.
  As you know, I'm a plagiarist . . .
Anyway, I am indifferent
 To failure . . . box with a triple
  Bottom . . . Time I confessed

XVII

At least to one crime: I write
 In invisible ink, and light   610
  Breaks only when it's reflected
In a glass. Since I am bereft
 All others, from this one road left
  I shall not quickly be deflected.

XVIII

If an angel had stooped in its flight
 Home to El Greco's heaven
  To explain to me wordlessly
But with a summer smile
 That more than all the seven
  Deadly sins he was forbidden me. 620

XIX

Then, if the unknown human
 Stepping out of the future
  Will impudently flash
His eyes and give to the flying
 Shade an armful of wet lilac
  In the hour when this storm has passed.

XX

But the century-old enchantress
   Suddenly woke up, felt like dancing,
     Making merry.   I'm at a loss.
Drops her lace handkerchief, languid   630
   Eyes look up from her stanzas,
     She gestures me across.

XXI

I've drunk of her, every drop,
   Didn't know how to stop
     The black thirst possessing me,
Binding me to her ravings:
   I threatened the Star Chamber,
     And drove her to her natal den—

XXII

To the darkness under Manfred's fir,
   And where Shelley, dead on the shore,   640
     Looked straight up into the sky,
While Byron held the brand, and
   All the world's skylarks shattered
     The dome beneath eternity.

XXIII

But she said in her most clear
   Voice: 'I am not that English muse,
     Not La Belle Dame Sans Merci;
July it was who brought me here,
   Except for the solar, the fabulous,
     I have no ancestry.   650

XXIV

But for all your equivocal glory
  Twenty years in the ditch, I
    Shall still not serve you thus,
But will compensate with a royal
  Kiss your wicked midnight.
    Sit, and feast with us.'

PART THREE

Epilogue

I love you, creation of Peter!

Pushkin: *The Bronze Horseman*

White night of 24 June 1942. The city in ruins. From the harbour to Smolny it is spread out to the gaze. Here and there old fires are burning themselves out. In the Sheremetyev Garden, limes are in flower and a nightingale is singing. A window on the third storey has been blown out, and behind it a black emptiness gapes. From the direction of Kronstadt heavy guns are audible. But generally it is quiet. Seven thousand kilometres away, the author's voice:

To my city

> Inside the House on the Fontanka
>   Where with a bunch of keys, a lantern,
>   The evening lassitude
> Begins, with an out-of-place laugh I   660
>   Hallooed to a distant echo, shattered
>   The unbroken sleep of things;
> Where, witness of all in the world,
>   At dawn or twilight, an old
>   Maple looks into the room

And, foreseeing my absence,
   Stretches out his dried and blackened
      Arm as if to help.
Earth hummed beneath my feet and
   The red planet was streaking   670
      Through my still unbroken roof.
It listened for its own password—that
   Sound that is all around us . . .
      And in Tobruk . . . it is everywhere.
You, not the first nor the last dark
   Auditor of bright madness,
      What vengeance do you prepare for me?
You will only sip, not drain to
   Its depths this bitter taste of
      Our separation.   Understand   680
There is no need to set your
   Hand upon my head.   Put an end to
      Time, let it forever remain
Here like a bookmark in a book at
   The silence of the cuckoo
      In the arson of our woods . . .

      And behind barbed wire
      In the dense taiga's heart
      —I don't know in what year
      Transformed to a pile of camp-dust, an   690
      Anecdote from the terrible fact—
      My double goes to interrogation,
      With two thugs sent by the Noseless Slut,
      And I hear from where I stand
      —Isn't that a miracle!—
      The sound of my own voice:
        I have paid for you in cash,
        For ten years I've looked
        Neither right nor left,
        Your ill fame at my back . . .   700

You, the grave I sprang from,
   Dearest, infernal, granite,
      Have paled, have died, lie still.

It's only imagined, our separation,
Nothing can split us, efface my
Shadow that's on your walls,
My reflection in your waters,
Steps in the Hermitage halls, where
My friend and I once strolled;
And in ancient Volkovo Field,   710
Where there's no end to weeping
The still fraternal graves.
All that the First Part said of
Love, betrayal and passion,
Free poetry brushes from its wings,
And my city is shrouded but standing . . .
Heavy are the slabs that
Press on your sleepless eyes,
Yet I dreamed in flight I heard you
Chase me, you who stayed to perish   720
In an iceblink of waters, a glitter of spires.
You did not wait for the beloved
Deliverers: a round-dance above you
Of brief white nights.
But the joyful word—home—
It is a word unknown to
All now, all look through foreign panes.
In New York, in Tashkent, the
Bitter air of exile
Is like a poisoned wine.   730
How admiringly you'd have watched me
As in the gut of the dolphin
I saved myself from the shark,
And over forests infested
Rushed like a witch's spectre
To the Brocken in the night.
And already the frozen Kama
Could be seen, and someone stammered
'Quo Vadis?' and before lips moved,
Another panorama,   740
With bridges and tunnels—the hammer
Of the Urals pounded below.

And under my eyes unravelled
  That road so many had travelled,
    By which they led away my son.
And that road was long—long—long, amidst the
  Solemn and crystal
                    Stillness
    Of Siberia's earth.
From all that to ash is rendered,   750
  Filled with mortal dread yet
    Knowing the calendar
Of vengeance, having wrung her
  Hands, her dry eyes lowered, Russia
    Walked before me towards the east.

Notes

Requiem

It was common practice with Akhmatova to subscribe, after a poem, the date, and sometimes place, of its composition. This information is provided below.

Quatrain. 1961.
Foreword. 'The Yezhov terror', or *yezhovshchina*, is the name Russians give to the worst period of the purges (1937–38), when Nikolai Yezhov was the official whom Stalin entrusted with the operation.
Dedication. March 1950.
1. 1935. In her memoir of Mandelstam, Akhmatova mentions that this poem refers to the arrest of her friend, Nikolai Punin, in 1935. He was released before the Yezhov terror began, and was not rearrested.
2. 'Husband clay' refers to Nikolai Gumilev, shot in 1921. In the original Russian, the last two lines have a peasant-like alliterative ferocity and simplicity that has, I think, eluded all translators.
3. This was published in a Moscow literary journal in 1966.
4. The original text mentions the name of the prison—Kresty (Crosses), perhaps with an allusion to its literal meaning.
5. 1939.
6. 1939.
7. 1939. Summer. This was printed, without title, as long ago as 1940, in the Leningrad literary journal *Zvezda*.
8. 19 August 1939, the House on the Fontanka. 'Police cap': the original has the 'blue cap' of the NKVD uniform. The Yenisei is a river in Siberia.
9. 4 May 1940, the House on the Fontanka.
10. 1940–43.

Epilogue. March 1940. 'Motionless bronze eyelids'—like the famous bronze equestrian statue of Peter the Great.

Poem without a Hero

Foreword

The epigraph is from the last stanza of *Eugene Onegin*. Pushkin takes farewell of his poem, and notes that many of his first readers are no longer around—including those hanged and exiled for their part in the Decembrist uprising. The aptness of the allusion needs no underlining.

'Certain absurd interpretations': many of Akhmatova's contemporaries criticised her for attacking the dead or people so far away they could not answer back.

Dedicatory poems

(1) Vs.K.—Vsevolod Knyazev. But the world of masks and doubles may already have started, for certain features of the poem strongly suggested to Nadezhda Mandelstam that the poem was really dedicated to her husband, who died in a Siberian transit-camp in 1938. 'After hearing Akhmatova recite her *Poem* for the first time in Tashkent, I asked to whom the "First Dedication" was addressed. "Whose first draft do you think I can write on?" she replied with some irritation. . . . I have two copies of the *Poem*. In one of them Knyazev's initials stand just above the "First Dedication", but have been crossed out by Akhmatova—she did this in my presence, saying it was a typing error. The other copy does not have his initials at all.' (Nadezhda Mandelstam: *Hope Abandoned*). If, as seems certain from other evidence too, Mandelstam and Knyazev are blurred together in the poem, they would appear to be mirror-reflections rather than doubles: the novice-poet who withdrew from life before the turmoil began, and the major poet who endured it all, to the anonymous mass-grave.

l. 8, 'Antinoüs': the allusion is probably to a favourite of the Emperor Hadrian, a youth of extraordinary beauty who drowned himself in the Nile in AD 130. Carl Proffer says it refers to the Homeric Antinoüs, braggart suitor to Penelope; but this seems less likely.

(2) O.A.G-S: Olga Glebova-Sudeikina. l. 17, 'blundering Psyche': literally Confusion-Psyche, one of her roles, in a play of the same name by Yury Belayev.

(3) A shadowy figure, presumably the 'guest from the future' (see l. 148, and note).

Part One, 1

l. 67, a quotation from Akhmatova's poem 'A New Year's Ballad', published in her collection *Anno Domini* (1921).

ll. 86–93. The masked guests who stream in are playing roles which were well known in the theatrical and literary life of Petersburg in those years. Don Juan recalls Mozart, Byron, Pushkin (*The Stone Guest*), Blok (*The Steps of the Commendatore*), but more immediately refers to Molière's version of the story, which was staged in 1910 by Vsevolod Meyerhold. 'Dapertutto' was Meyerhold's commedia dell'arte pen name. John the Baptist—from Richard Strauss's opera, based on Wilde's *Salome*, and also a ballet by Fokine. Glahn is a character in Knut Hansun's *Pan*. The 'goatlegged nymph' is Sudeikina: late in 1912 she danced a ballet called *The Fauns*. A contemporary photograph shows her in the costume of a faun, with goat's horns.

l. 94, 'the walls have widened': symbolically, to all Russia.

l. 112, 'The Prince of Darkness': Mikhail Kuzmin.

l. 132, 'the valley of God's anger': the Day of Judgment.

ll. 142–49. This passage was inspired by an actual visitor from the West, Isaiah Berlin, who came to see Akhmatova not long after the war. Under the conditions that prevailed, she regarded the visit as providential, almost literally 'from the future'. In reality, the Soviet authorities used it as one of their excuses for the renewed imprisonment of her son and persecution of herself. Max Hayward points out her extreme precision of detail: to reach her apartment in a wing of the old Sheremetyev Palace, it would have been necessary to turn left from a bridge over the Fontanka canal.

ll. 163–64, 'You come in the motley stripes/Of a milepost': this passage is about Blok. The striped milepost is a feature of the Russian landscape. Blok stands, a tragi-farcical figure, on the border of the nineteenth and twentieth centuries, between Tsarism and Communism.

l. 165, 'old as the Mamre/Oak': see Genesis xiv, 13, 24.

l. 182, 'Poets are blind to sin': Nadezhda Mandelstam has stressed that what fundamentally distinguished the Acmeists from the Symbolists was moral concern. 'The Acmeists renounced the cult of the poet and the principle that "all is permitted" to the man who "dares".' (*Hope Abandoned*)

l. 216, '*I am ready for death*': words spoken by Mandelstam to Akhmatova three months before his first arrest, for writing an anti-Stalinist poem, in 1934. The identities of Knyazev and Mandelstam are again blurred.

ll. 224–26. These lines, as B. A. Fillipov points out, are clearly inspired by the description of Kirillov in Dostoyevsky's *Possessed*, after he had hanged himself: 'In the corner formed by the wall and the cupboard, Kirillov was standing—and standing in a terribly strange manner.'

Across the Landing
Like Hedda Gabler's, Knyazev's suicide is an astonishing and irritating intrusion upon the busy scene, which is dominated by Sudeikina in her wild dance.

ll. 238–40, 'Isaac's': St Isaac's Square; 'the Dog': the Stray Dog.

l. 257, 'the head of Madame de Lamballe': the title of a famous poem by M. Voloshin, written in 1906, about a victim of the French Revolution.

l. 264, 'oceanic dance': the Russian adjective is 'okayanniy' (cursed); the pull of the English word, oceanic, which echoes the sound so closely, proved too much for this translator to swim against.

l. 271, 'Ivanushka of the fable' is a familiar character in Russian folklore. Usually, while his two bright brothers get married and get on, he sits on the stove and catches flies.

Part One, 2
Besides the goatlegged nymph, all the other roles mentioned in the introductory passage were associated with Sudeikina. Her husband painted her portrait in the role of the blunderer (Confusion-Psyche).

l. 283, 'Meyerhold's blackamoors': Meyerhold's production of Molière's *Don Juan* opened with a swarm of slave boys running on stage, lighting candles, ringing bells, etc.

l. 286, 'flayed the hide of the nation': Peter the Great built Petersburg on a swamp, at enormous cost in human lives.

ll. 291–304. The glory of Petersburg's musical and theatrical life is evoked, through the reference to Anna Pavlova dancing the Swan (Saint-Saëns–Fokine) at the famous Mariinsky Theatre; and to Chaliapin.

l. 306, 'the twelve colleges' corridor': the corridor of Leningrad University is noted for its exceptional length (1,500 feet).

Originally the building, begun by Peter the Great, housed twelve ministries ('colleges'). The poet, writing with her 'invisible ink', is doubtless alluding to the Soviet brand of education and culture —monolithic, 'straight'.

ll. 310–17. Akhmatova visited Paris in the spring of 1911, when Stravinsky's *Petrushka* was performed by the Ballets Russes and created a sensation. The ballet was performed in Petersburg in 1913. The 'yellow-black flag' is the imperial standard. The Summer Garden is the city's central park, beside the Neva. Tsushima is an island off Japan, where the Russian fleet was annihilated in 1905.

ll. 320–41. The shadows fly and Blok ('Mephistophilis or Gabriel') holds the stage alone. 'Demon with the smile of Tamara' refers to Lermontov's romantic poem, *Demon*; Tamara, a Gretchen figure, is destroyed by the Demon's kiss, but her soul is taken to heaven by an angel. Blok himself relates his gift of a black rose in his short poem, *In the Restaurant*; and reality and art are again confused in the reference to his Don Juan poem, *The Steps of the Commendatore*, which is a close parallel to the reality of Knyazev's entrance into the heroine's house before his suicide.

l. 355, 'O my blond-haired wonder'. Nadezhda Mandelstam's impression of her, ten years later: 'A nice, light-headed, flighty creature who had suffered much from hunger and other ordeals during the terrible years of Revolution.' (*Hope Abandoned*)

l. 365, the 'protected cedar' was at Komarovo, near Leningrad, a place much loved by Akhmatova. It is there that she is buried.

l. 370, the 'Maltese chapel' is in the former palace of the Vorontsovs in Leningrad.

Part One, 3

The poem's historical dimension is powerfully visualised in this section: the ominous approach of 'the existing/Twentieth Century' (i.e. from 1914).

ll. 440–53. The Cameron Gallery is a building at Tsarskoye Selo. 'All nine' refers to the nine muses. This tender reminiscence is addressed (according to Carl Proffer) to the critic N. V. Nedobrovo, Akhmatova's first love. It could equally be addressed to Gumilev.

Part One, 4

Mars Field is a large open area by the Neva, used for military parades. The house built by the brothers Adamini was one that

Akhmatova lived in for some years in the 1920s. The Church of the Saviour on the Blood was built in the late nineteenth century on the spot where Tsar Alexander II was assassinated. The church became a centre for anti-totalitarian thought in the period after the Revolution.

l. 471, 'On the road back from Damascus': Sudeikina was involved in a performance of a play called 'The Road from Damascus' at the Stray Dog. She is returning home from the cabaret with Blok. This is an excellent example of the fusion of literal precision and parable in the poem: for it is also a return into sin, as if St Paul changed back into Saul.

Part Two
Epigraph: 'My future is in my past'. Akhmatova's notebook refers to T. S. Eliot as the source. Shortly before her death she is said to have learnt that it was the motto of Mary Queen of Scots. It is intriguing that Akhmatova must have known Eliot's *Four Quartets*, in view of the similarities between the works: the musical form, the concern with time and history and the timeless soul; much of both works was written in cities under siege. That Akhmatova felt deeply for London's plight is attested by her poem *To the Londoners*: 'Time is now writing with impassive hand/ Shakespeare's black play, his twenty-fourth/ . . . Only not this one, not this one, not this one—/ This one we do not have the strength to read.' Eliot's poem is Akhmatova's English 'double'.

The reference, in the introduction, to *Requiem* first appears in one of the author's last revisions, near the end of her life.

l. 525, 'There were three': Blok, Kuzmin, Knyazev. Carl Proffer suggests Sudeikina, Blok, Knyazev, surely a gross misreading since clearly the first two must be celebrated poets.

l. 541, 'soft embalmer': this phrase, from Keats' sonnet *To Sleep*, is quoted in English in the Russian text.

l. 549. The Satanic figure is, again, Kuzmin (cf. ll. 109–19). Three poems by Kuzmin may provide a clue to his role in Knyazev's suicide. They are homosexual love poems to a young man, and two of them are dedicated to 'V.K.'. Both of these poems were written in 1912. The third poem, 'In sad and pale make-up', is addressed to a 'blond Pierrot' (cf. l. 393), whom the poet wishes to kiss endlessly. It is dated 1912–13. Beside any part he may have played in Knyazev's suicide, Akhmatova evidently finds his attitude towards it intolerable.

l. 561. Akhmatova's seventh book of poetry went with her in her evacuation from Leningrad during the siege. It never appeared in print. In the same plane was Shostakovich, with the score of his seventh symphony, 'the Leningrad'. B. A. Fillipov comments that the allusion may also encompass Beethoven's Seventh, which Akhmatova deeply loved. Once again, the deliberate blurring and mirror-effect is evident.

ll. 567–69, 579–84. In a note, Akhmatova writes—perhaps ironically—that the omitted stanzas are in imitation of Pushkin: who did indeed suppress stanzas for political reasons. The truth may be, I suggest, that originally the Soviet censors demanded cuts here before they would allow publication. We know that cuts were demanded—not surprisingly—in Parts Two and Three; she refused to publish these parts under such conditions. Perhaps later she saw how artistically effective these hiatuses could be. In them, 'silence itself speaks'.

ll. 595–96: Luga is a town near Leningrad; 'the land of the satin half mask' is Venice.

l. 601. *White Flock* and *Plantain* are early books by Akhmatova.

ll. 627–56. The author is for a moment afraid that her poem, which so obsesses her, is only another creation of the Romantic muse, that 'century-old enchantress'. But the muse protests that she has no ancestors. Despite the abundance of literary and artistic allusions, *Poem without a Hero* is, as Max Hayward has said, 'a conscious attempt to go beyond the Romantic poem. . . . Her main purpose is to recall an era in which there were no more heroes, only pseudo-Romantic masqueraders; the hero-individualist of the nineteenth century has come to the end of the road and his epigones (unless, like Knyazev, they died young) would be offered up wholesale to the Moloch of war and revolution.' Similarly the poem is not, as has been suggested, a regression to Symbolism: Symbolism 'was rooted, at the best, only in the imagination of its representatives. Akhmatova, on the other hand, was speaking not from imagination only, but from the depth of unimaginable experience.'

Part Three

ll. 687–700. Akhmatova's last double in the poem is mysterious. It is everyone who has perished in the labour-camps. But it is also her son, almost certainly: she does not know in what year he will suffer the most normal fate in those circumstances, death. She may also have in mind, again, her great friend and peer,

Mandelstam. Exactly when Mandelstam perished is uncertain to this day, though his widow believes it to be 27 December 1938. And Akhmatova's closeness and loyalty to him was remarkable; his death could not weaken the bond. 'We shouldn't be viewed as twins,' she used to say, 'but neither can we be separated: we go together.' For eighteen years, she and Nadezhda Mandelstam alone kept his poetry alive.

l. 693, 'the Noseless Slut': an obscure reference, perhaps death in the Stalinist era, faceless and indiscriminate.

l. 708, 'Hermitage halls': the Hermitage Museum of Art.

Appendix:

Three lyrics from the time of the 'Petersburg masquerade'

Evening

Sorrow's own music in the garden.
The sea breathes pungently, freshly,
From oysters in a dish of ice.
He said, 'I am your true friend!'
And let his hand fall on my dress.

Well, it wasn't an embrace exactly . . .
More like the way you'd stroke a cat
Or let your glance linger on a bare-back rider!
I couldn't see anything in his eyes,
Except laughter.

And the violins kept singing with such sorrow:
'Give thanks, give thanks to God:
You are alone with him at last.'

1913

Don't conceive me trampled by riots
Of regret, aching all through.
But nor does my soul deny its
Insignificant meeting with you.

Red house I pass by on purpose,
Red house by the muddy stream,
But I know that I bitterly disturb
Your sun-pervaded dream.

Though it was not you who hovered,
Craving love, over my mouth,
Though it was not your golden verses
Which immortalised my youth—

I sometimes cast spells on the future,
When the evenings are cloudlessly blue,
And foretell a second meeting,
Unavoidable meeting, with you.

1913

I dream of him more rarely now,
See him, thank God, now less than everywhere.
A mist has settled on the white road,
Shadows flit across the water.   The ploughed-

Up earth's expanse has borne all day
Chime upon chime of monastery bells.
Here are St Jonas' bells best heard,
Its belfries gleaming distantly.

Lilac-branches that have shed their last
Blossom surrender to my pruning-shears.
Along the top of the ancient battlements
Two monks have slowly passed.

Bring to life before my blinded eyes
The clear, familiar, material world.
The King of Heaven has healed my raw soul
With the calm numbness of a carapace.

1914

9 780804 011952